# Love Doesn't Just Die — Intimacy Fades, and Love Gets Blamed

## Why Couples Think They've Fallen Out of Love and How to Restore What's Missing

OLAJUMOKE JANET ADETUNJI

WWW. INTIMACYAWAKEN.COM

E-book ISBN 978-978-68-6986-5

Print ISBN: 978-978-68-6987-2

All Scripture quotations, unless otherwise indicated are taken from the Niv version of the Bible.



If you enjoy this book, please consider leaving a review.

Thank You!

# Dedication

This book is dedicated to every couple who still loves each other but feels disconnected and to God who restores intimacy, heals what feels broken, and brings hearts back together.

# Contents

# Acknowledgments

This book would not exist without God; the Author of love, the Restorer of intimacy, and the One who continues to redeem what feels broken. Thank You, Lord, for being patient with us, for showing us what covenant love truly looks like, and for reminding us that what You create, You also sustain when we invite You in.

To my husband, Tayo; thank you for loving me in real life, not just in theory. Thank you for continuously walking through growth, discomfort, laughter, hard conversations, healing, and grace with me. Our marriage has been both a classroom and a sanctuary, and I am grateful that we continue choosing each other, even when it's not easy.

To my beautiful daughters, Esther, and Elizabeth; you are a constant reminder of why healthy love matters. May you always know that intimacy, safety, faith, and connection are worth protecting and pursuing.

To every couple I've had the honor of coaching, counseling, and walking alongside. Thank you for trusting me with your stories. Your honesty, pain, courage, and willingness to try again shaped this book more than you know. You taught me that love doesn't disappear overnight. It slowly goes quiet when intimacy is neglected, misunderstood, or wounded.

To the faith leaders, mentors, teachers, and counselors who poured into me spiritually and professionally, thank you for grounding truth in grace and wisdom in compassion.

To friends and loved ones, who have supported and encouraged me to write this book and continue my coaching practice. Thank you for your support and presence.

And to you, the reader, thank you for being here. If you read this book and complete the reflections and next steps, it means you still care. It means there is something in you that hopes things can be better, deeper, safer, and more connected. That alone tells me love isn't dead in your story. My prayer is that by reading this book, you will begin to get clarity that restoration is possible, intimacy can be rebuilt, and love, when rooted in truth, faith, and intentional connection, can be awakened again.

# Foreword

In my more than 30 years of ministry, I have had the privilege of presiding over one hundred weddings. I count it a sacred responsibility to stand with a couple on the first day of their life together as they make their vows before God, surrounded by family and friends.

When a man and a woman are joined together in marriage, they enter into a covenant established by God Himself. They make promises—to love, honor, and cherish one another in all circumstances. ***And I believe them***. I believe in the sincerity of their vows and their desire to remain faithful for as long as they both shall live.

That is why it is both confusing and heartbreaking when, just a few years later, some of these same couples sit across from me and say, "We're not in love anymore." Naturally, I ask, "What happened?" Often, the answer is the same: "We don't know. We just drifted apart. We don't feel the way we used to."

There is a deep sadness in those moments. Many of these couples know the love of Jesus. Many genuinely want to love each other. And yet, love feels distant—exhausting… even impossible.

**Can you relate?** You may have heard the advice, "You need to work on your marriage." But what does that really mean? Try harder? Do more? Fix your feelings?

In *Love Doesn't Just Die*, Janet Adetunji offers a different and much-needed perspective. This is *not* a call to try harder. Instead, she helps us recognize that we often misdiagnose the problem. What appears to be a failure of love is often a breakdown of intimacy.

From a Christian perspective, this makes sense. Sin does not simply affect us individually; it destroys our relationships. It turns us inward, away from one another, and away from God and the self-giving love designed for marriage. Left unchecked, that drift slowly erodes even the strongest relationships.

But God does not leave us there. In Christ, God not only forgives our sin, but he restores our relationship with him. We enjoy peace with God and a close and intimate relationship. King David gives us a glimpse of this kind of intimate relationship in Psalm 139.

[1] ***"You have searched me, Lord, and you know me.***
[2] ***You know when I sit and when I rise;***
***you perceive my thoughts from afar.***
[3] ***You discern my going out and my lying down;***
***you are familiar with all my ways.***
[4] ***Before a word is on my tongue***
***you, Lord, know it completely."*** **Psalm 139:1-4**

The God who knows you completely and loves you unconditionally, allows you to draw on his love as you create intimacy in your marriage. Now, take a deep breath. Today is a new day. Take your first steps, together, on a journey toward the intimacy God desires for you.

*Pastor Dan Solofra - Sr Pastor Crosswalk Church, Laveen AZ*

# Introduction

*"I don't think I love you anymore"* –

Many people say this quietly. Some say it in anger. Some say it with tears. But most people do not understand what they actually mean.

When someone says, "I don't love you anymore," what they are usually describing isn't the death of love. It's the absence of closeness. It's emotional exhaustion. It's years of unmet needs, unspoken disappointments, and feeling unseen in the very place that was supposed to feel safe. **But Love doesn't just die.**

The opposite of love is hate, and hate takes effort. Abuse takes intent. Deep resentment takes repeated harm.

Most marriages without physical and emotional abuse don't reach that place of hate. Couples simply drift and get too exhausted to keep trying.

They get busy. They get tired. They stop talking beyond logistics and chores. They stop touching each other without a reason. They stop checking in emotionally. And one day, they wake up next to someone they're committed to but no longer feel close to.

Then they assume the worst: ***"We must have fallen out of love."***

This book is here to gently tell you something different. **What you lost wasn't love. You lost intimacy.**

And **intimacy can be awakened again**.

## How This Book Helps You

This book is not meant to be read in a rush. It's meant to be felt, reflected on, and returned to. As you read, you'll notice that this isn't a book about fixing your spouse or forcing emotions back into place. It's about understanding what happened beneath the surface and learning how to move toward each other again without pressure or fear.

Throughout these pages, you will be gently guided through what I call the "Intimacy Awakening Path." Not as a rigid system, but as a way of seeing clearly and choosing intentionally.

First, you'll begin to understand the drift (The Quiet Drift). You'll see why intimacy fades quietly in good marriages, and why what you're feeling doesn't mean love has died.

Then, you'll learn how safety weakens (The Safety Breakdown); emotionally, physically, and spiritually, because intimacy cannot grow where people feel guarded, exhausted, or misunderstood. Most importantly, having an understanding that God needs to be the center of your marriage, for it to truly thrive.

Then you will learn how to restore safety without pressure or performance (The Gentle Repair). Finally, you'll be invited to choose closeness again (The intentional Return), not perfectly, not dramatically, but faithfully. Through small, intentional moments that reopen connection over time.

This book is not asking you to do everything at once. It's asking you to start somewhere. You don't need to feel hopeful before you begin, you just need to be willing. **No shame. No blame. No pressure.** Just clarity, hope, and a way forward.

**NOTE:** If your relationship includes physical abuse, ongoing harm, or destructive addictive behaviors that are not being addressed, you require more than the steps in these pages.

Your next steps require **support, safety, and professional or pastoral guidance**. You do not have to navigate that alone.

Seeking help is not a sign of failure, it is a step toward protection, clarity, and healing.

"**LOVE** - the bond created through time, shared life, memories, and commitment, doesn't just vanish, it just struggles to express itself."

# The Quiet Drift

## *Faded Intimacy ≠ Death of Love*

# *Chapter 1*

## Love Doesn't Just Die. It Goes Quiet

Some couples believe love ends suddenly. That one day, something snaps, feelings disappear, and a marriage collapses under the weight of "irreconcilable differences" and "no longer in love." But that is rarely how love just disappears.

Love doesn't usually die in a dramatic moment. It fades quietly. It fades in the spaces between conversations that no longer happen. In the exhaustion that leaves little room for emotional presence. In the unresolved hurts that are set aside because life feels too busy to deal with them properly.

## When Love Is Still There, But Connection Is Not

This is one of the most confusing places to be in a marriage. You still function well as a couple. You manage schedules, children, responsibilities, and church commitments. From the outside, everything looks fine. But inside the relationship, something feels quieter than it used to be. Conversations are polite or not, touch is occasional, emotional closeness feels optional rather than natural.

Nothing is broken, nothing dramatic has happened. This is often where intimacy just begins to fade, unnoticed and unnamed.

This is what I call **"The Quiet Drift."**

## The Slow Quiet Drift Most Couples Don't Notice

Disconnection doesn't usually announce itself. It settles in gradually. It grows when emotional needs go unspoken, misunderstandings go unresolved, fatigue becomes a constant companion, responsibilities increase, children demand more, work stretches longer. The mental and emotional load of daily life grows heavier, and somewhere along the way, emotional presence begins to thin out.

Not because love is gone, but because energy is limited and you cannot be bothered.

This is how intimacy quietly weakens. Not through betrayal or cruelty, but through neglect that was never intentional.

**Why This Feels So Confusing**

One of the most difficult parts of this stage is that couples often sense the distance but struggle to explain it or have a resolution.

There may be no major conflict. No obvious crisis. Just a growing sense of distance that doesn't match how much you still care, and couples end up blaming themselves. They assume they've failed. They wonder if something is wrong with them.

They question whether their love was ever real to begin with. Some even begin to think their spouse is cheating. But what's happening is not the death of love. It's an emotional drift. A slow and quiet weakening of the connections that once made the relationship feel alive.

**Love Needs More Than Commitment to Stay Alive**

At this point, we begin to feel love is fragile but that is far from reality. Love is resilient, feelings are fragile, attraction can fluctuate and desire can disappear for seasons, but Intimacy requires presence. Presence requires emotional availability. And emotional availability requires safety, trust, and intentional care.

When those elements slowly disappear. LOVE - the bond created through time, shared life, memories, and commitment, doesn't just vanish, it just struggles to express itself.

This is why couples can still love each other deeply and yet feel painfully disconnected at the same time because **Intimacy has weakened.**

This is where you **pause and reflect honestly (without blame)** - Reflection is not about figuring out who failed. **It's**

**about noticing patterns, not assigning faults but naming the drift**, so restoration becomes possible.

**Ask Yourself This:**

- When did my marriage stop feeling emotionally close, not dramatic, just distant?
- What pressures or responsibilities increased during that season?
- Where have we been surviving instead of truly connecting?

**What to Do Next (Small Actions That Matter)**

- **Name the drift:** Within the next 24 hours, write or think through this sentence. No editing, no justifying, not who caused it, not how to fix it. Just when and what changed.

"Our marriage started feeling emotionally distant when ---------"

This creates clarity. You can't reconnect to what you can't name.

- Respond to the drift with one intentional awareness conversation with your spouse. No long discussion, no rehashing history, just a signal of awareness and care.

Example: *"I've been reflecting lately and I realized that somewhere along the way, we stopped connecting after* ***["Named Drift"].*** *I'm not blaming you. I just want to say it out loud because you matter to me and I don't want to ignore it anymore. I would like us to revive the connection."*

**Prayer Prompt**

"God, help us recognize the quiet drift before it becomes deep distance. Open our eyes to where we stopped connecting.

Give us the courage to name what changed without blaming each other and teach us how to move toward each other again. In Jesus name, Amen."

**"Sex is an expression of intimacy, not the definition of it.**

**Intimacy is the experience of being known, seen, chosen, and emotionally connected to another person."**

# The Quiet Drift

*Intimacy ≠ Sex*

# *Chapter 2*

## Intimacy Is More Than Sex

For many couples, intimacy and sex are often used interchangeably, so, before we go any further, I need to clarify one thing. **Intimacy is more than sex.**

Sex is an expression of intimacy, not the definition of it. When intimacy is reduced to physical connection alone, couples may find themselves confused, especially when sex no longer brings the closeness it once did. Also, sex can happen without intimacy. Intimacy, however, cannot thrive without intentional care.

## Understanding Intimacy Beyond Physical

Intimacy is the experience of being known, seen, chosen, and emotionally connected to another person. It involves trust, vulnerability, and emotional safety. It is built through shared moments of honesty without fear, meaningful conversations, touch that comforts without pressure, sexual satisfaction, spiritual connection, and the sense that you are emotionally and physically safe with one another, even during disagreement. It is what makes love feel alive.

When intimacy fades, love starts to feel distant, dull, or even nonexistent. That's why when people say, *"I love you, but I'm not in love with you,"* what they're really saying is:

> "I don't feel close to you anymore.," "I don't feel seen."
>
> …

And instead of addressing the loss of intimacy, couples panic about the loss of love. This misdiagnosis is dangerous. Because when people believe love is gone, they stop trying, they withdraw, they emotionally detach, they start imagining life elsewhere, where connection might feel easier.

But the moment there is self-awareness, everything changes. Because you're no longer asking, "Is our marriage over?" You're asking, ***"Where did we lose closeness, and how do we restore it?"***

That's a much safer, more hopeful question.

Throughout this book, when we talk about intimacy, we are talking about the **quality of connection** between two people: emotionally, physically, intellectually, and spiritually.

**Pause & Reflect: Ask Yourself This:**

- How do I define intimacy in my marriage?
- Do I feel emotionally connected to my spouse right now?
- In what ways might we be expecting sex to meet emotional needs?

**Next Step**

This week, focus on emotional connection rather than physical outcomes.

- Create space for conversation.
- Offer attention without expectation.
- Practice presence without pressure.

When intimacy is nurtured emotionally and built spiritually, physical closeness often follows naturally.

**Prayer Prompt**

"Lord, teach us what true intimacy really means. Help us to stop reducing connection to performance. Restore emotional closeness in our marriage and let our physical intimacy grow from safety, not pressure. In Jesus name, Amen."

"Argument says, "This matter" and you're reaching for each other.

Distance says, "I don't know how to reach you anymore."

**Distance isn't peace. It's often unaddressed hurt that becomes silence."**

# The Quiet Drift

*Distance ≠ Peace*

# *Chapter 3*

# How Couples Slowly Lose Intimacy

We've established that intimacy rarely disappears because of one big moment. It fades one decision at a time and in ordinary things. It happens gradually, quietly, almost invisibly, while life keeps moving.

**Here are some reasons intimacy slowly declines:**

## Intimacy Begins To Fade When Connection Is Repeatedly Postponed.

Life becomes busy. Work gets demanding, Children need more attention, bills and chores pile up and energy runs low.

Conversations become practical instead of personal. "Did you pay the bill?," "What's for dinner?," "Can you pick up the kids?"

Nothing is wrong with any of this, but affection is delayed, not intentionally withheld. It is quietly placed on hold, for when things slow down. But as you know, things rarely slow down.

Over time, couples begin to operate more as roommates or partners managing life than as two people emotionally connected to each other. The relationship still functions, but something vital feels missing.

Everything appears fine on the surface. But really, intimacy has quietly taken a back seat.

**Intimacy Fades After Series of Unspoken Expectations and Disappointments.**

Small hurts that never get addressed don't disappear. They settle. They create emotional caution. Over time, couples stop sharing honestly, not because they don't care, but because it feels safer not to share.

So instead of saying, "I feel hurt," people say nothing.

Instead of saying, "I miss you," they stay busy.

Instead of saying, "I need your help," they silently feel disappointed and stay overwhelmed.

Instead of saying, "I feel lonely," they withdraw.

This is how emotional distance grows without an argument.

**Intimacy Also Fades When Couples Choose Distance Over Argument and Truth.**

Rather than arguing, some couples choose to avoid conflict by choosing distance or their version of "peace." Of course, we all want peace but not at the expense of honesty and truth. Avoiding conflict can feel loving in the moment, but unresolved tension quietly builds walls and when honesty disappears, closeness soon follows. Let me explain why argument, if done in a healthy manner, is a safer choice than choosing distance.

**Argument vs Distance**

Arguments can be messy (not in an abusive kind of way), but distance is quiet. Argument says, "this matter." Distance says, "I don't know how to reach you anymore." Argument still means you're reaching for each other.

Most couples drift apart, not because they fight too much. They drifted apart because they stopped reaching and fighting fair.

**Distance makes you invisible:** In argument, you are still seen- even if its messy. In distance, your thoughts, feelings, and needs go unnoticed.

**Distance removes hope quietly:** Arguments carry the belief that something can change. Distance carries resignation. No raised voices, No tension, just emotional resignation. That to me is heavier and ready to be labeled "irreconcilable differences."

**Distance teaches you to self-protect:** When argument stops, people don't suddenly feel safer. They learn how to shrink, withhold, and manage themselves. You stop saying what you feel. You stop asking for what you need and stop expecting repair.

**Distance kills desire without drama:** Desire needs emotional presence. Arguments still have presence. But distance removes energy, curiosity, and pursuit, not through rejection but through absence.

**Distance rewrites the relationship story:** Argument says: "we are struggling." Distance says: "this is just how it is now." And once people accept that story, they stop trying to change it. And label it "We've fallen out of love."

**Distance isn't peace. It's often unaddressed hurt that becomes silence.**

**Another Common Intimacy Killer Is Exhaustion.**

When you're tired, overwhelmed, or emotionally drained, connection feels like work. Couples don't stop loving each other, they stop having the energy to engage or initiate. And the most dangerous part is that most couples don't notice until the distance feels uncomfortable. By then, they're not just disconnected, they're confused. They start wondering and asking these questions:

*"Why don't I feel close anymore?"*

*"Why don't I feel the spark anymore?"*

*"Why does it feel easier to be on my phone than with my spouse?"*

The truth is simple but sobering. Intimacy is not maintained automatically. It fades when it's unattended and rarely restores itself without attention and intentionality.

**Intimacy Requires Intention and Attention**

Intimacy is sustained through consistent emotional presence. It grows when couples make space for one another, not only physically, but emotionally and spiritually.

When that space slowly disappears, intimacy weakens.

This does not mean the marriage is failing. It means the connection needs care and intimacy needs to be awakened.

Recognizing this early can prevent distance from becoming disconnection.

**Pause And Reflect-** Which one sounds most like your marriage right now. Busyness, postponed conversations, unresolved tension, unspoken hurt, conflict avoidance, or exhaustion?

**Ask Yourself Truly –** Not with criticism but out of curiosity.

- When life got busy, what stopped happening between us?
- What did I stop expressing because it felt easier not to?
- Where did I choose silence instead of honesty?

**What to Do Next (Small Actions That Matter)**

You don't fix drifting with grand gestures. You reverse it with **intentional presence**.

Choose one action to begin closing those gaps:

- One honest conversation this week (no fixing, just sharing)
- One moment of undistracted attention each day
- One emotional check-in: "How are you really doing lately?"

Change begins when intimacy becomes intentional again. These actions are not meant to fix everything. They are meant to interrupt the drift.

**Prayer Prompt**

"God, reveal the small places where we've postponed connection.

Show us where silence replaced honesty. Help us choose presence over distance. In Jesus name, Amen."

**"Emotional safety is not the absence of conflict, but the presence of trust. It is knowing that you can express a thought, a fear, or a desire without being mocked, dismissed, minimized, gaslighted, or punished for it."**

# The Safety Breakdown

*Emotional Safety ≠ Lack of Conflict*

# *Chapter 4*

## When Emotional Safety Begins to Weaken

By this point, many couples are no longer just tired, they are emotionally guarded. They may still want closeness, but something inside feels hesitant.

It stops feeling safe to be fully honest, vulnerability feels harder. You hesitate before speaking because you're not sure how your words will land. You avoid certain topics to keep the peace and avoid conflict. Even affection can feel complicated – loaded with expectations or misunderstanding.

The issue isn't lack of love; it's lack of emotional safety. When emotional safety weakens, intimacy levels begin to drop. This is the stage I call **"The Safety Breakdown."**

Nothing dramatic may have happened. There may not have been a major betrayal or crisis. But small moments have added up including emotional fatigue. Over time, the relationship no longer feels like the safest place.

**What Emotional Safety Really Means**

Emotional safety is not the absence of conflict, but the presence of trust. It is knowing that you can express a thought, a fear, or a desire without being mocked, dismissed, minimized, gaslighted, or punished for it. It's feeling confident that it will be received with care, even when they are difficult to hear.

In emotionally safe relationships: Feelings are allowed, even when they are uncomfortable. Conflict is addressed, not avoided or weaponized. Mistakes are met with curiosity and sincere apologies, not contempt or defensiveness. Vulnerability is protected, not exploited.

Safety isn't built by being perfect. It's built by being willing to repair. Repair matters more than perfection. Small moments of repair helps to rebuild trust:

"I didn't mean it that way." "I can see how that hurts you." "I'm sorry, I was defensive."

These moments and simple words reopen the door to closeness.

When emotional safety is strong, intimacy flows more naturally. When it weakens, people begin to guard themselves, not out of selfishness, but out of self-protection.

## The Role of Exhaustion and Overload

For many couples, emotional safety doesn't break down during arguments. It breaks down in the ordinary rhythms of daily life and a home that never quite rests.

When one partner feels consistently overwhelmed, carrying the weight of the householding, the children's schedules, the emotional labor of remembering, planning, and anticipating. Something subtle begins to happen in the midst of exhaustion. Resentment grows quietly, connection feels like another demand. Intimacy becomes exhausting instead of life-giving.

Emotional safety includes knowing that you are not alone in the work of life and this is not about keeping score but about feeling supported.

Over time, one or both partners begin to shut down emotionally after multiple tries where conversations feel one-sided, repeated defensiveness occurs instead of understanding, apologies that never quite repair the hurt or seem sincere and conflict that ends with silence instead of resolution. Sharing feels exhausting. Explaining feels pointless.

It seems safer to just keep the peace than to risk another misunderstanding. This is not emotional immaturity. It's a nervous system responding to repeated emotional strain. This is a tough spot to be in a marriage.

## Guardedness Is a Signal, Not a Failure

It's important to say this clearly: Becoming emotionally guarded does not mean your marriage is broken. It means something needs attention.

Guardedness is a signal that repair is needed, not more effort, not more pressure, and certainly not more guilt. When couples try to push intimacy forward without circling back to restore safety, it often backfires.

One partner feels pressured, the other feels rejected, and the distance grows. Both are hurting. Both feel misunderstood.

In the case where help and partnership are missing, what's often heard is not: *"You didn't wash the dishes."* What's felt is "I'm carrying this by myself." The exhaustion shuts down desire.

The feeling of being overwhelmed reduces emotional availability. Over time, this creates emotional distance. The partner who is exhausted may feel unseen or unappreciated and may think: *"I don't have anything left to give."* The other partner may think *"I don't know how to reach you anymore."* Neither is wrong. But without emotional safety, expressed through care, help, and shared responsibility, intimacy becomes a pressure instead of a pleasure, not because love is gone, but because energy is depleted.

This is the point where intimacy cannot be restored by effort alone. This is why emotional safety must include **practical partnership** and be rebuilt through understanding, gentleness, and friendship.

**When Words Become Wounds: The Silent Destruction of Emotional Safety**

Emotional Safety can be weakened slowly through words that are spoken carelessly, repeatedly, and without intentional and sincere repair.

Verbal abuse is not always loud or obvious. Sometimes it sounds like sarcasm that cuts a little too deep, belittling comments, name-calling, or words spoken in anger that are never taken back. Over time, these words don't just hurt in the moment, they begin to shape how your spouse sees themselves.

A person who is consistently spoken down to does not remain the same. Their confidence begins to shrink. They start second-guessing themselves. They may withdraw, shut down, or stop expressing their needs altogether; not because they don't have anything to say, but because they no longer feel safe.

And then something happens. There is a breaking point.

The same person who has been quiet, patient, or enduring suddenly reacts in a way that seems "out of character." They snap. They push back or emotionally disengage. Not because they are unstable, but because they have reached their mental capacity or what their heart can carry.

This is what repeated verbal harm does. It doesn't just create conflict; it weakens the foundation of safety that intimacy needs to survive. The scripture speaks clearly about the power of our words:

[12]***"The tongue has the power of life and death, and those who love it will eat its fruit"*** **- Proverb 18:21**

[18]***"The words of the reckless pierce like swords, but the tongue of the wise brings healing"*** **- Proverbs 12:18**

[29]***"Do not let any unwholesome talk come out of your mouths, but only what is helpful for building others up according to their needs, that it may benefit those who listen"*** **- Ephesians 4:29**

Your words are not neutral. They are either building your spouse up or slowly tearing them down.

In marriages, the tongue can become a weapon – or it can become a building tool. Every harsh word chips away at emotional safety.

Every cutting remark teaches your spouse, *"You are not safe with me."* And once safety is weakened, intimacy doesn't just struggle. It begins to fade.

But the same tongue that wounds also have the power to heal.

A shift in how we speak, choosing gentleness over harshness, understanding over attack, and repair over silence. This can begin to rebuild what was broken. It won't happen instantly, but it will happen intentionally. Don't be afraid to also seek professional counselling or therapy in the healing process.

If this chapter of the book lands close to home. Understand this, God designed marriage to be a safe haven and partnership, not a burden carried by one while the other watches from the side or where one tears the other down.

**Pause and Reflect** - Take a moment and sit with these questions.

- Do I feel supported in the daily work of life and parenting?
- Does my spouse feel supported by me?
- Where might exhaustion be affecting our emotional connection?
- Do I feel emotionally safe expressing my needs and frustrations in this relationship?
- When my spouse hears my voice, do they feel safe or do they brace themselves?
- Are there topics I avoid because they tend to lead to conflict or shutdown?
- When conflict happens, do we usually repair them, or do they stay unresolved?

Notice what comes up without judging yourself or your spouse. Awareness is the beginning of restoration.

**What to Do Next (Small Actions That Matter)**

Restore One Small Area of Safety. This week, choose one small way to restore emotional safety. Not a big conversation or confrontation. Just one intentional shift

It could look like:

- Listening without interrupting, correcting, or defending.
- Share one honest thought or experience from your day.
- Acknowledging your spouse's feelings.
- Offering a sincere apology where repair was missed.
- Creating space for a calm, harm-free conversation.
- Pray for your spouse. Speak life and build up.
- Giving your spouse uninterrupted rest.
- Initiating help without being asked.

Intimacy does not return through urgency. It returns where safety is rebuilt, one small, faithful step at a time.

**Prayer Prompt**

"God, help us reconnect. Help us feel safe with each other again and let the words we say to each other build and bring life. Help me to be a true partner to my spouse and provide a safe haven for our home. In Jesus name, Amen."

**"When someone doesn't feel emotionally safe or feel mentally drained or constantly unsatisfied sexually, desire struggles to show up and "lack of desire" is frequently treated as the problem."**

# The Safety Breakdown

## *Sexless ≠ Desireless*

# *Chapter 5*

## When Emotional Distance Reaches The Bedroom

Emotional disconnection often shows up in the bedroom long before couples recognize it anywhere else. When someone doesn't feel wanted outside the bedroom, they stop wanting inside it. For some couples, sex becomes routine and mechanical. It becomes rare, tense, or avoided altogether. And for others, it feels disconnected, like something happening around them rather than between them.

This is often the point where couples begin to worry. Not because love is gone, but because something that once felt natural and passionate now feels distant or nonexistent.

### How Emotional Distance Shows Up Physically

The truth is this: **Sex doesn't create intimacy, intimacy fuels sexual desire.** Intimacy is the emotional safety that allows desire to flourish. Without that foundation, sex often starts to feel like pressure, duty, or obligation rather than connection and something passionate.

That's why many couples touch less long before they stop having sex. Hugs disappear, casual affection fades, playfulness quiets down. Touch can begin to feel loaded, carrying expectations and pressure. And when touch loses safety, desire retreats.

What was once affectionate may now feel complicated. Even small gestures can feel emotionally risky when closeness no longer feels safe.

Sexual desire may fade, not because attraction has disappeared, but because emotional connection has weakened. The body often responds to emotional distance long before the mind fully understands what is happening.

This is why many couples are surprised by changes in their sex life. They didn't consciously choose distance or celibacy.

It arrived quietly, through layers of busyness, unaddressed emotions, and unmet needs.

**Desire Is Often Blamed, but Rarely Understood**

Couples blame themselves or each other for sexual distance when the real issue is emotional disconnect. Sometimes, it isn't about attractiveness, libido, or effort. It's about connections.

When someone doesn't feel emotionally safe or feel mentally drained or constantly unsatisfied sexually, desire struggles to show up and "lack of desire" is frequently treated as the problem.

But desire is deeply responsive. It is influenced by stress levels, exhaustion, continuous sexual dissatisfaction, emotional safety, and unresolved tension. When these factors are present, sexual desire naturally retreats, not as a punishment, but as a form of self-protection.

Many couples try to fix a lack of sexual desire without addressing the emotional environment in which it exists.

This is where many couples feel stuck, leading to frustration, pressure, and further disconnection.

**Two People, Two Different Experiences**

Often, each partner responds from a different emotional place.

One partner may long for physical closeness as a way to restore connection - *"If we just had more sex, we'd feel closer."* Sex feels like reassurance, affirmation, and a return to what once felt secure.

The other partner may need emotional closeness before physical intimacy feels safe or desirable - *"I don't feel close enough to want sex."* Without that foundation, sexual advances can feel overwhelming or pressured, even when love is still present.

Both experiences are valid and come from a desire to feel connected. It is about two people responding to intimacy from different emotional needs and levels of safety. Neither belief tells the full story, but both feel real. Without awareness, couples often personalize these differences instead of understanding them.

This dynamic can leave couples feeling frustrated, discouraged, or even disconnected further. Neither feels emotionally safe enough to bridge the gap alone.

**How Misunderstanding Deepens the Distance**

When these needs are not recognized, couples can unintentionally hurt each other. The partner seeking physical closeness may feel rejected or unwanted. The partner needing emotional safety may feel misunderstood or pressured.

Over time, this dynamic creates a cycle of frustration. One reaches forward while the other pulls back. Each response reinforces the other's fear.

Rebuilding sexual intimacy starts by removing pressure and it grows when couples:

- Feel heard without defensiveness!

- Experience affection and partnership without expectation.
- Selflessly seek to pleasure their spouse than receiving
- Feel chosen without performance.

**Having Sex Even When You Don't Feel Like It.**

Now here is another truth, while sex doesn't create intimacy, it can still support it. Some people believe: *"If I don't feel emotionally close, I shouldn't have sex."* This is where many couples also get stuck, leading to a sexless marriage.

Not that I approve, but the reality is people have sex with strangers, without any form of emotional intimacy. Which means sex in itself is not dependent on deep connection to occur.

And here's an important truth: **You "can" choose sex with your spouse even when you are not happy or in the mood,** not to pretend everything is fine, but to benefit from what sex provides.

Having regular sex with your spouse can:

- Reduce stress levels!
- Lower emotional wall!
- Create a moment of closeness!
- Provide a safer space to talk and listen afterward!

For some couples, **sex becomes the bridge back to conversation**, not the reward for fixing everything first.

This doesn't mean ignoring hurt or forcing yourself. It means understanding that sex can also be a rebuilding tool, not just a result.

The key question is not: "Do I feel like it? But: **"What would choosing closeness right now make possible?"** Wisdom is knowing what choice takes you closer to rebuilding intimacy.

The goal is not obligation, but intentional closeness, chosen with wisdom, consent, and care.

**Pause and reflect with discernment -** Has sex in your marriage changed because intimacy faded or has intimacy faded because sex became difficult?

**Ask yourself this**:

- Am I avoiding sex because I feel emotionally unsafe or because I'm waiting to feel perfect again?
- In moments of disconnection, what am I most afraid of losing?
- Could choosing closeness open a door to healing?
- What might my spouse be experiencing that I have not fully considered?

**What to Do Next (Small Actions That Matter)**

- Get to understand your spouse emotional and sexual needs and levels of safety. Also Share your sexual desires and boundaries with your spouse

  **Want:** What am I excited about, what turns me on, what will get me to an orgasm?

**Will:** I would be willing to try these activities but not entirely comfortable with them. Let us proceed on my own terms.

**Wont:** Currently, I am unwilling to participate in these activities. Here is why …... Please do not pressure or ask me. I will let you know if anything changes.

- Choose one daily moment of intentional togetherness this week. No agenda, no fixing, just presence:
    - Sitting together without phones, cuddled up, even in silence.
    - Doing something small (like flirtatious cooking) together.
    - Reintroduce safe touch without expectation, hug longer than usual, cuddle without pressure and try the "60 second kiss".

These moments may feel insignificant, but they slowly restore emotional familiarity. Consistency matters more than creativity. Let your body relearn safety before desire.

**Prayer Prompt**

"Father, heal the places where intimacy feels tense or distant. Remove shame, pressure, and misunderstanding from our sex life. Restore desire and help us to be selfless in pleasuring each other.

Teach us how to choose closeness with wisdom, consent, and love. In Jesus name, Amen."

"Marriage is a house built over time, shaped by seasons, and tested by storms. When God is removed from the foundation, couples are left carrying weight they were never meant to carry alone. **Effort without God leads to exhaustion. Partnership with God leads to stability.**"

# The Gentle Repair

*Partnership with God*
*= Safety & Stability*

# *Chapter 6*

# The Quiet Cost of Neglecting Spiritual Intimacy

For many couples, intimacy doesn't just fade because of conflict, it fades because God is no longer the center of their home, instead they have quietly moved God to the background. Not intentionally, not rebelliously, just slowly.

They may still attend church, believe in the same things, and pray individually. Yet something feels different.

What once felt shared now feels separate. Spiritual practices that once connected the marriage begin to feel individual, inconsistent, or absent altogether.

Prayers become private instead of shared. Faith becomes siloed instead of united. God is invited into church or problems but not into conversations, decisions, emotions, or their sex life.

### How Spiritual Distance Quietly Develops

When couples stop praying together, a spiritual drift occurs and they often stop seeing each other through God's grace. Patience shortens, assumptions grow and emotional closeness weakens. Over time the marriage still functions, but the spiritual covering thins out. Not out of sin, but out of disconnection. And when spiritual intimacy fades, emotional and physical intimacy often follow.

### Why God Must Be at the Center

There is one truth that must be told clearly. Marriage was never designed to be sustained by two people alone. God designed intimacy to be meaningful and connected through Him.

When couples try to carry emotional connection, healing, forgiveness, and intimacy solely on their own strength and feelings, exhaustion is inevitable. Love begins to feel heavy instead of life-giving.

God is not a last resort in marriage repair. He is the center that holds it together. When you submit your marriage, your hurt, your confusion, your desire for closeness and sexual satisfaction to God, you remove the pressure to fix everything perfectly. You invite grace into the process. You allow God to become the cord that binds you together in safety, patience, and love.

***[1]"Unless the Lord builds the house, the builders labor in vain."- Psalm 127:1***

Marriage is a house built over time, shaped by seasons, and tested by storms. When God is removed from the foundation, couples are left carrying weight they were never meant to carry alone.

This verse reminds us of a freeing truth: **Effort without God leads to exhaustion. Partnership with God leads to stability.**

This is the stage I call **"The Gentle Repair."** Inviting God into your marriage is not a weakness. It is wisdom. Restoration deepens when God is invited into the work, not as a judge, but as a healer and a connector.

**Pause And Reflect With Discernment** - Sit with these questions gently and notice what surfaces without rushing to fix it

- How often do we invite God into our marriage together, not just individually?
- When challenges arise, do we turn to God as a couple or separately?
- What do I miss about how we once connected spiritually?
- When last did we study the bible together as a couple or family?
- When last did I ask God to spice up our sex life?

**What to Do Next (Small Actions That Matter)**

Choose one small act of spiritual reconnection, not a routine, not a rule, but habit building.

- Say a brief prayer together once a week and let the habit grow.
- Study a bible passage together and share what God is teaching you.
- Pray for sexual intimacy growth.
- Begin the repair with an awareness conversation.

Example: *"I've been thinking about how little we pray together lately. I'm not trying to make any drastic change in our schedule right now. I just miss sharing that part of our spiritual journey with you and hope we can ask God to help revive it."*

**Prayer Prompt**

"Father, somewhere along the way, we stopped inviting You into our marriage the way we once did. Not out of rebellion… just busyness, tiredness, and routine. But we acknowledge your importance in our lives and marriage. Draw us back to You, and back to each other.

Teach us to pray together again and help us see each other through your lens. Help us seek You not only in crisis, but in connection. Restore the spiritual closeness we've neglected and be the center of this marriage again.

In Jesus name, Amen."

"You don't repair intimacy by fixing everything. You repair it by first identifying where safety and intimacy weakened, whether emotionally, physically, or spiritually, so you know where to begin."

# The Gentle Repair

*Awareness is the Foundation*

# *Chapter 7*

# Intimacy Awakening Begins With Awareness

Intimacy awakening does not begin with change. It begins with awareness. Before closeness can be restored, couples must first recognize what has been lost, how it happened, and what has been hiding under the marriage iceberg. Without awareness, efforts to reconnect often feel forced or short-lived.

This stage invites honesty rather than urgency. Understanding where intimacy broke helps couples stop guessing and start healing.

**Seeing the Relationship Clearly**

Awareness requires couples to look at their relationship without blame or defensiveness. It means acknowledging distance without assigning faults and recognizing patterns without judgment.

If you are a couple with little children that requires every moment of your day and unintentionally the drifting begins. Acknowledging that this is a phase in your life, recognizing the schedule patterns, and intentionally creating space for each other begins the rebuilding process.

This is not about revisiting every past hurt. It is about noticing what has been happening quietly and consistently over time. It is also about self-reflection. Not finding ways to blame your spouse.

When couples become aware of these patterns, intimacy begins to shift, not because anything has been fixed yet, but because understanding has replaced confusion.

**Why Awareness Can Feel Uncomfortable**

Awareness often brings discomfort. It can surface emotions that were previously ignored or minimized. It may reveal areas of neglect, exhaustion, or unmet needs that feel difficult to face.

As you begin your awareness journey, invite God to journey with you and help you manage your emotions and response to the discomfort.

Discomfort is not the same as danger. So don't let the influx of awareness bring you back to the point of *"I don't think I can do this anymore."*

Awareness creates space for compassion, both for yourself and for your spouse. It allows couples to respond with curiosity instead of defensiveness, and patience instead of pressure.

In the awakening process, awareness is not the final step, it is the foundation. Without it, attempts at change tend to repeat old patterns. With it, couples can begin addressing intimacy with intention rather than reaction.

This stage is about slowing down enough to truly see what is present, instead of rushing toward what is missing.

**Letting Awareness Lead, Not Fear**

When intimacy has been strained for a long time, fear often drives the desire for change. Fear of losing connection. Fear of growing further apart. Fear that it may be too late. At this point, couples attempt to fix intimacy through effort alone; more conversations, more attempts at sex, or more pressure to "get back to normal."

Let the awareness gently interrupt fear. Let it shift the focus from fixing to understanding, and from pressure to presence.

This is where healing begins, not with effort, but with clarity.

**What's needed is not force, but intentionality and insight.**

The key insight? You don't repair intimacy by fixing everything. You repair it by first identifying where safety and intimacy weakened, whether emotionally, physically, or spiritually, so you know where to begin.

**Pause and reflect -** Take a moment to reflect:

- What patterns have been repeated in our relationship over time?
- Where have we felt stuck or unsure how to move forward?
- What emotions surface as I become more aware of our intimacy?
- When did we last enjoy each other's company without distraction?
- What moments do I reserve for others but not my spouse?
- Where have I chosen efficiency over togetherness?

**What to do next:** This week, choose awareness over action.

- Notice moments of connection and disconnection without trying to change them immediately.
- Pay attention to you and your spouse's emotional responses, with curiosity rather than judgment.

Awareness creates the conditions for intimacy to awaken naturally.

**Prayer Prompt**

"God, show me where intimacy needs attention, manage my emotions and remove the need to avoid the hard truths. Teach me how to choose closeness with wisdom, patience, and grace.

In Jesus name, Amen."

> **"Feelings fluctuate with stress, seasons, hormones, responsibilities, and unresolved emotions. Waiting for feelings to lead can keep couples stuck for years."**

# The Intentional Return

*Intimacy does not require perfection*

# *Chapter 8*

## Choosing To Awaken Intimacy

Awakening intimacy is not about returning to the past. It is about choosing to move forward with greater awareness, compassion, and intention.

By now, you may recognize parts of your own marriage in these pages. Moments of distance. Seasons of confusion. Areas where connections quietly weakened. This recognition is not meant to bring guilt or regret but understanding. Understanding opens the door to change. I call this stage **"The Intentional Return."**

## Choosing Intimacy Even When Feelings Lag

This is an invitation to choose closeness even when emotions are slow to follow. I know this seems like a tough ask, but it is possible.

One of the myths in marriage is that **intimacy should feel natural all the time. It doesn't.**

Feelings fluctuate with stress, seasons, hormones, responsibilities, and unresolved emotions. Waiting for feelings to lead can keep couples stuck for years. Mature intimacy understands this truth:

Sometimes intimacy follows feelings and sometimes feelings follow intimacy. Choosing intimacy does not mean ignoring pain or pretending everything is fine. It means deciding that connection matters more than your ego.

This choice looks like:

- Showing up even when it feels awkward.
- Initiating physical intimacy even when unsure of the response.

- Staying engaged instead of withdrawing.
- Asking for what you need, even if you feel it's obvious.

Many couples wait for motivation before acting. But sometimes motivation often comes after action. This is why small, consistent choices matter more than emotional intensity.

Choosing intimacy also means giving each other grace during the process. There will be missteps. There will be awkward moments. There will be times when effort isn't reciprocated immediately.

This does not mean it isn't working. It means intimacy is being rebuilt. Meet your spouse where they are and watch the trust and safety grow.

**What Awakening Intimacy Really Requires**

Awakening intimacy does not require perfection. It does not demand that everything be resolved at once. It begins with small, intentional choices made consistently over time.

It asks for honesty instead of avoidance. Presence instead of pressure. Compassion and self-reflection instead of blaming. These choices create space for intimacy to return not all at once, but gradually, as safety and trust are rebuilt.

**When Progress Feels Slow**

For many couples, healing does not feel dramatic. It feels subtle.

There may be progress followed by setbacks. Moments of connection followed by distance. This does not mean the process isn't working. Growth rarely follows a straight line. What matters is the willingness to stay present and engaged, even when change feels slow.

**You Are Not Alone in This Journey**

Many couples assume they are the only ones struggling in this way. But loss of intimacy is common, and so is restoration. They compare their private distance to others' public closeness and quietly conclude they have failed or they want what someone else has. The grass is not always greener on the other side and if it is, they water and tend to it. Make an intentional choice to tend to your marriage and rebuild or nurture intimacy.

Choosing to awaken intimacy is not an admission of weakness. It is an act of courage and hope.

**Moving Forward with Intention**

As you move forward, remember that intimacy is not sustained by grand gestures, but by consistent care, paying attention, listening, supporting each other, shared vulnerability, true partnership, selflessness and placing it all in God's hands. These are the building blocks of a connected marriage.

**Pause & Reflect**

Take a moment to reflect:

- What has become clearer to me through this journey?
- What am I willing to do differently moving forward?

- Where do I feel hopeful, even if change feels uncertain?

**Next Step:** Choose one intention you will carry forward from this book. Not a goal to perfect, just a posture to practice.

Let curiosity, patience, or presence guide how you show up in your relationship. Most importantly bring God back into your intimate spaces including your sex life.

Intimacy awakens where attention remains and intentionality exists.

**Prayer Prompt**

"God, give us the courage to choose intimacy even when feelings lag. Help us act with intention instead of waiting for perfection.

Strengthen our willingness to stay engaged in the rebuilding process and let our small steps lead to lasting connection.

In Jesus name, Amen."

"Healing in marriage is rarely loud or dramatic. It is quiet, steady, and deeply sacred. It took time for intimacy to fade; it is going to take some time to rebuild.

And that is okay."

# The Intentional Return

*Consistency & Intentionality is key*

# *Closing Chapter*

## Love Was Never the Problem

This book was never meant to be the end of your intimacy building journey. It's the beginning of a new way of relating, choosing, and reconnecting.

If you have made it this far, take a moment and breathe. Not because everything is suddenly fixed, but because something important has shifted.

You are no longer panicking about whether your marriage is over.

You are no longer assuming the worst about your love story.

You are no longer carrying the weight of believing something has died. You now realize that ***Lack of Love was never the problem.***

What you experienced was distance.

What you felt was disconnection.

What you interpreted as loss was unattended intimacy.

And that matters because intimacy can be rebuilt.

This book was never about making you try harder or do more. It was about helping you see clearly, choose intentionally, and moving gently toward closeness again.

Some days, reconnection will feel natural. Other days, it will feel awkward or slow. Both are normal.

Healing in marriage is rarely loud or dramatic. It is quiet, steady, and deeply sacred. It took time for intimacy to fade; it is going to take some time to rebuild. And that is okay.

**Where God Comes In**

This is where many couples feel both relief and permission. You were never meant to repair your marriage alone.

God is not standing outside your marriage waiting for perfection. He is within it, offering grace when patience runs thin, wisdom when emotions are high, and strength when you feel exhausted.

Submitting your marriage to God is not giving up responsibility. It is releasing control. It is saying:

- "We need You."
- "Lead us where we don't know how to go."
- "Teach us how to love when feelings feel weak."
- Be the center of our marriage.

**Let Go of the pressure.**

You don't have to fix everything at once.

You don't have to feel hopeful every day.

You don't have to get it right immediately.

What you need is willingness. The willingness to reach instead of retreating.

Willingness to choose closeness, even when it feels unfamiliar.

Willingness to please your spouse, without expecting anything in return.

Willingness to invite God into the spaces where you feel tender and unsure.

Small, faithful steps matter. An honest conversation, sincere apology, a gentle touch, a moment of prayer at the end of a long day, spoken or silent. These are seeds of intimacy.

Your marriage does not need to return to what it once was. It can grow into something deeper. More honest, intentional, sexually satisfying and spiritually grounded.

Love matures when intimacy is cared for with grace. It flourishes when God is not an afterthought, but the foundation and center.

**You are not alone.**

Remember, you are not too far gone, your marriage isn't broken beyond repair, and you are not alone.

Love isn't dead. Intimacy can be awakened and with God at the center, restoration is not just possible, it is promised.

The bible reminds us that a cord of three strands is not easily broken: husband, wife, and God. When God becomes that third strand, he creates an avenue for safety to replace fear, patience to soften frustration, and tenderness returns where walls had formed.

He becomes a steady presence holding space for restoration.

***12"Though one may be overpowered, two can defend themselves. A cord of three strands is not quickly broken."***

**- Ecclesiastes 4:12**

This is the promise your marriage stands on. Not perfection, not constant happiness, not flawless communication, but connection strengthened by God's presence.

When God becomes the third strand, love gains resilience, intimacy gains safety, and hope gains roots.

**A Final Invitation:** Before you close this book, pause. Place your marriage, the confusion, hurt, pain, grief, and hope, exactly as it is, into God's hands.

Not a polished version. All of it; the good, bad, and ugly.

**Prayer Prompt:**

"God, we invite You fully into our marriage.

Be our foundation and awaken intimacy within us.

Heal what we do not understand.

Help us choose love, even when it feels quiet.

Be the cord that binds us together again. In Jesus name. Amen!"

# A Gentle Invitation

If this book helped you name what has been happening in your marriage, you may already feel one thing clearly: understanding is the beginning but not always the end.

Some couples can take the next steps on their own. Others require guidance, structure, or support as they rebuild connection. If you find yourself wanting help in applying what you've read, in a way that feels safe and respectful, and at your pace, you don't have to figure that out alone.

Through coaching, courses, or guided resources, I work with couples who want to restore emotional closeness, rebuild trust, and awaken intimacy. To help you take the next step in rebuilding closeness in your marriage, download the free "Relationship Reflection guide for Couples." www.intimacyawaken.com/LDJD-Resource - A marriage closeness assessment, Conversation prompts for couples and a simple intimacy rebuilding exercise designed to help you continue the journey, just practical tools to move forward together.

# About The Author

**Olajumoke Janet Adetunji - Relationship, Sex & Intimacy Coach**

*Certified Sexologist (ABS), Certified Love Coach, Certified Master Sexpert, Certified Relationship Coach, Prepare-Enrich Facilitator with Biblical Counseling Degree*

Olajumoke Janet Adetunji is a certified Relationship, Sex, and Intimacy Coach and a certified Sexologist dedicated to helping couples build emotionally safe, spiritually grounded, and sexually fulfilling marriages.

As a child of God, a wife, mother to two beautiful daughters, and the founder of Intimacy Awakening Coaching LLC, she understands some of the marital challenges that couples and families face. Her mission is simple: to empower and equip couples with practical tips, tools, and resources to help navigate the journey of marriage and intimacy, enhance communication, conflict resolution skills, revive passion without shame or pressure, and create a safe environment to call home. Her work blends relationship science with biblical principles, offering couples a balanced and sustainable path to healing and growth.

Olajumoke specializes in guiding couples through emotional disconnection, sexual intimacy challenges, and marital conflict, helping them move from distance to deep connection. Her approach is compassionate, clear, personalized and solution driven.

You deserve a vibrant, fulfilling love life, and she is excited to guide you on this journey.

Made in the USA
Coppell, TX
12 July 2026

84078949R00056